First Facts™

Health Matters

Flu

by Jason Glaser

Consultant:
James R. Hubbard, MD
Fellow in the American Academy of Pediatrics
Iowa Medical Society
West Des Moines, Iowa

Capstone
press

Mankato, Minnesota

First Facts is published by Capstone Press,
151 Good Counsel Drive, P.O. Box 669, Mankato, Minnesota 56002.
www.capstonepress.com

Library of Congress Cataloging-in-Publication Data
Glaser, Jason.
    Flu / by Jason Glaser.
    p. cm.—(First facts. Health matters)
    Summary: "Introduces the flu, its symptoms, treatments, and prevention"
—Provided by publisher.
    Includes bibliographical references and index.
    ISBN 0-7368-4290-X (hardcover)
    1. Influenza—Juvenile literature. I. Title. II. Series.
RC150.G56 2006
616.2'03—dc22   2004031052

Editorial Credits
Mari C. Schuh, editor; Juliette Peters, designer; Kelly Garvin, photo researcher/photo editor

Photo Credits
BananaStock, Ltd., 1, 5 (inset)
Capstone Press/Karon Dubke, cover (foreground), 8, 9, 10, 11, 15
Corbis, 20; Paul Barton, 6–7; Walter Hodges, 16–17
Creatas, 12–13
Getty Images Inc./Peter Cade, 14; Taxi/Richard Price, 19
Photo Researchers Inc./Science Photo Library/NIBSC, cover (background)
RubberBall Productions, 21
Visuals Unlimited/Science VU/CDC, 5 (background)

Table of Contents

What Is the Flu?

The flu, or influenza, is an illness caused by a **virus**. A virus is a tiny germ. Flu viruses copy themselves over and over inside your body. As your body fights the virus, you will feel achy.

Fact!
People get the flu from three kinds of viruses.

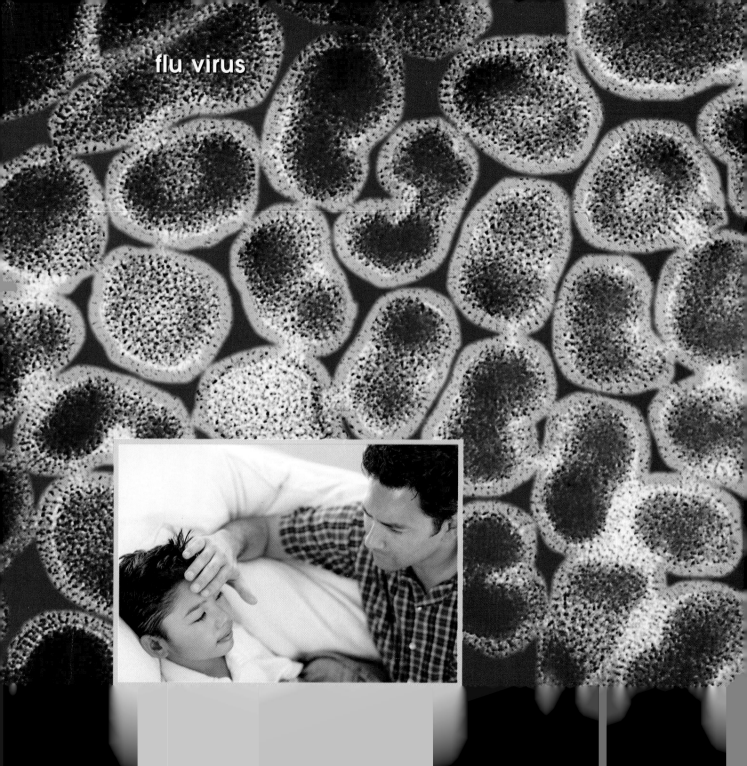

flu virus

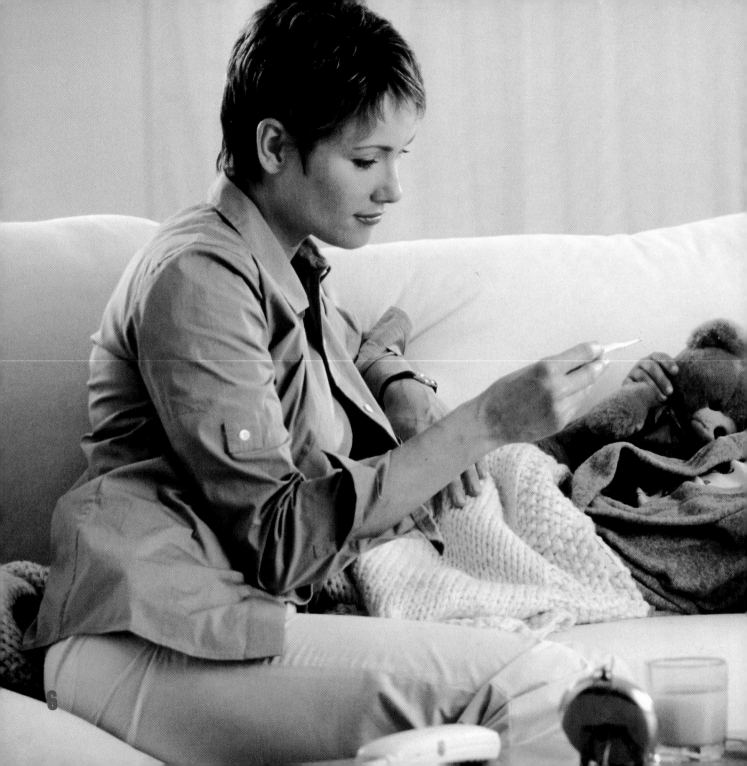

Signs of the Flu

People with the flu often have muscle pain and **fever**. The flu makes people feel hot, then cold.

The flu also has other signs. People often cough and have runny noses. People with the flu often feel very tired. They may have a headache and a sore throat. They might not feel like eating.

How Do Kids Get the Flu?

People with the flu sneeze, cough, and breathe viruses into the air. Then other people get the flu by breathing in these flu viruses.

Flu viruses are also spread by touching people who have the flu. The virus gets inside the body when people touch their mouth, nose, or eyes.

What Else Could It Be?

Many illnesses have signs like the flu. Colds cause sore throats and runny noses. Strep throat causes fever and a sore throat.

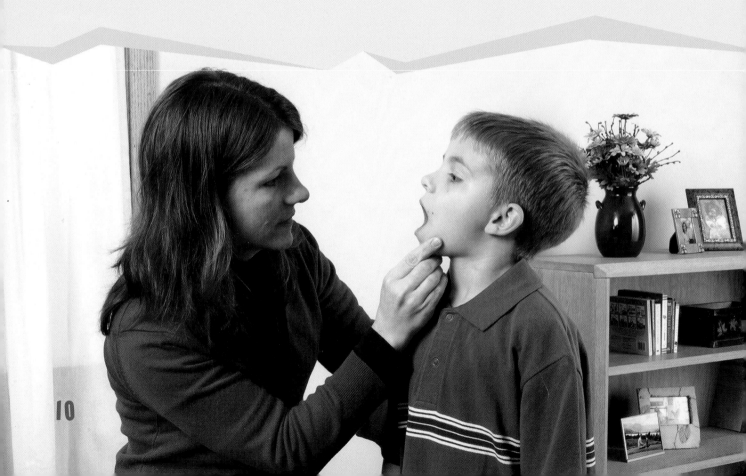

People with stomach flu have
stomach pains and may throw up. Germs
that cause stomach flu are different from
the germs that cause the flu.

Should Kids See a Doctor?

Kids with the flu usually should see a doctor. The flu can hurt the body and cause other illnesses. Doctors use **medicine** to help people with the flu feel better.

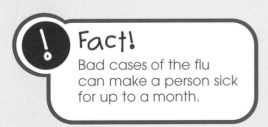

Fact!
Bad cases of the flu can make a person sick for up to a month.

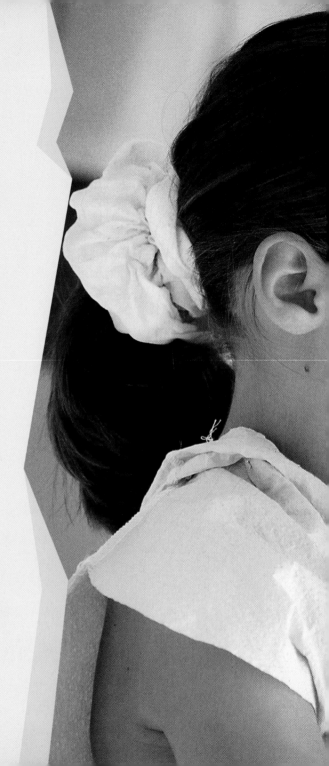

How to Treat the Flu

People with the flu need lots of rest. They should stay home so other people don't get the flu. People with the flu should drink lots of water.

Some things treat signs of the flu. Adults can give kids safe medicine for pain. **Gargling** with salt water helps a sore throat.

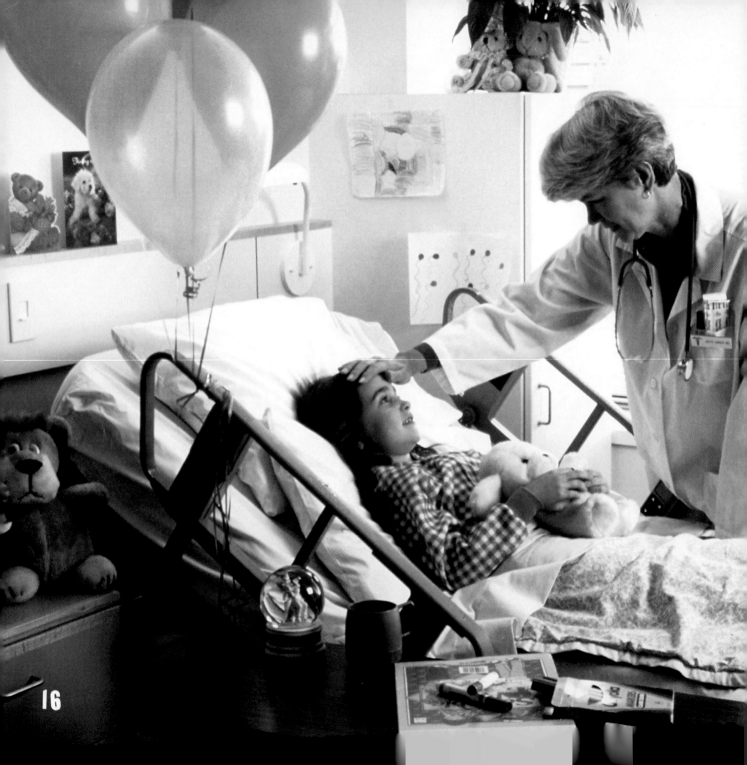

If It Gets Worse

If the flu gets worse, a person can get **pneumonia**. This illness makes breathing difficult. People with pneumonia can die.

The flu can also lead to bronchitis. People with bronchitis cough and **wheeze**.

 Fact!
People who have had the flu usually don't catch it again for a year.

17

Staying Healthy

Preventing the flu is possible. Most people can get a shot to help prevent the flu. Washing hands with soap and warm water can kill flu viruses on skin. People also can stay away from people who have the flu.

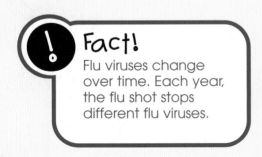

Fact!
Flu viruses change over time. Each year, the flu shot stops different flu viruses.

Amazing but True!

The worst flu outbreak in history began in Spain in 1918. The "Spanish Flu" killed at least 20 million people around the world in only six months. This number of people is equal to everyone living in the state of Texas today.

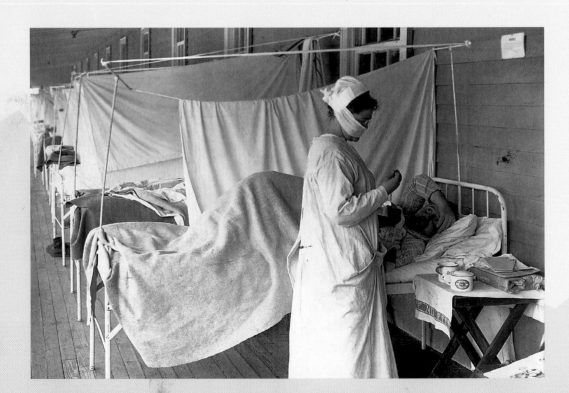

Hands On: Virus Tag

Many diseases can be spread by touch. Try this activity to learn how viruses can spread.

What You Need

three or more friends
a large open space to run

What You Do

1. Choose one person to be "the virus."
2. Have that person raise his or her hand in the air.
3. The virus tries to tag other players.
4. The other players try to keep from being tagged.
5. Anyone tagged also becomes a "virus" and raises one hand.
6. The new viruses also try to tag runners.
7. Keep playing until everyone becomes a virus.

This game shows how quickly a virus can copy itself and take over healthy cells. Viruses like the flu spread slowly early on. But after viruses make many copies, they spread very quickly.

Glossary

fever (FEE-vur)—a body temperature that is higher than normal

gargle (GAR-guhl)—to move a liquid around in the back of your throat without swallowing it

medicine (MED-uh-suhn)—pills or syrup that can make people feel better during illness

pneumonia (noo-MOH-nyuh)—a serious illness that makes the lungs fill with thick fluid; people with pneumonia have a hard time breathing.

virus (VY-russ)—a germ that copies itself inside the body's cells

wheeze (WEEZ)—to have a hard time breathing, making a whistling noise in your chest

Read More

Feeney, Kathy. *Sleep Well: Why You Need to Rest.* Your Health. Mankato, Minn.: Bridgestone Books, 2002.

Isle, Mick. *Everything You Need to Know about Colds and Flu.* The Need to Know Library. New York: Rosen, 2000.

Laskey, Elizabeth. *Flu.* It's Catching. Chicago: Heinemann Library, 2003.

Internet Sites

FactHound offers a safe, fun way to find Internet sites related to this book. All of the sites on FactHound have been researched by our staff.

Here's how:
1. Visit *www.facthound.com*
2. Type in this special code **073684290X** for age-appropriate sites. Or enter a search word related to this book for a more general search.
3. Click on the **Fetch It** button.

FactHound will fetch the best sites for you!

Index